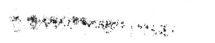

SINKHOLES

Megan Kopp

www.av2books.com

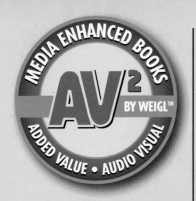

MEDIA ENHANCED BOOKS
AV²
BY WEIGL™
ADDED VALUE • AUDIO VISUAL

AV² provides enriched content that supplements and complements this book. Weigl's AV² books strive to create inspired learning and engage young minds in a total learning experience.

Your AV² Media Enhanced books come alive with...

Audio
Listen to sections of the book read aloud.

Key Words
Study vocabulary, and complete a matching word activity.

Go to **www.av2books.com**, and enter this book's unique code.

Video
Watch informative video clips.

Quizzes
Test your knowledge.

BOOK CODE

N958443

Embedded Weblinks
Gain additional information for research.

Slide Show
View images and captions, and prepare a presentation.

AV² by Weigl brings you media enhanced books that support active learning.

Try This!
Complete activities and hands-on experiments.

... and much, much more!

Published by AV² by Weigl
350 5th Avenue, 59th Floor
New York, NY 10118

Website: www.av2books.com   www.weigl.com

Library of Congress Control Number: 2013940588
ISBN 978-1-62127-955-6
ISBN 978-1-62127-956-3

Printed in the United States of America in North Mankato, Minnesota
1 2 3 4 5 6 7 8 9 0 17 16 15 14 13

062013
WEP220513

Editor Pamela Dell
Project Coordinator Aaron Carr
Art Director Mandy Christiansen

Photo Credits
Every reasonable effort has been made to trace ownership and to obtain permission to reprint copyright material. The publishers would be pleased to have any errors or omissions brought to their attention so that they may be corrected in subsequent printings.

Weigl acknowledges Alamy, Corbis, and Getty Images as its primary image supplier for this title.

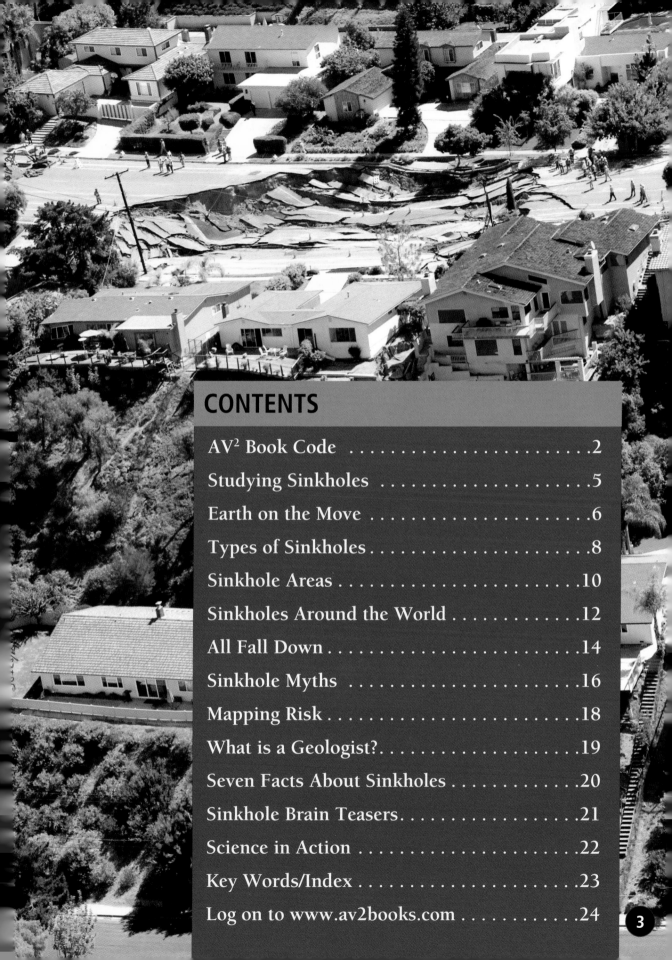

CONTENTS

In 2010, a huge sinkhole opened up in the ground at the center of Guatemala City, Guatemala. Measuring 59 feet (18 meters) wide and 328 feet (100 m) deep, it swallowed a three-story building. Scientists believe the sinkhole developed after rain washed out the underground drainage system.

Studying Sinkholes

Sinkholes happen all around the world. They mostly form through natural processes. Human activity can also cause sinkholes, although some geologists do not consider these true sinkholes. These scientists believe sinkholes caused by people should be called something different to distinguish them from those that happen naturally.

A sinkhole begins underground. It may show up simply as a slump in the earth's surface, like a shallow bowl. If the empty space underground grows too large, however, the ground above it may collapse completely, often without warning. Big sinkholes that open suddenly can cause roads to crack and buildings to collapse. In rare cases, people may fall into sinkholes that open up beneath them.

Geologists and other scientists use special tools to study sinkholes. They study how sinkholes form and what causes them. They examine underground rock and soil and study the flow of underground water. These scientists use what they learn to try to **predict** where sinkholes may occur. Predicting sinkholes is a difficult job.

■ Sinkholes occur in a variety of shapes from steep-walled "natural wells" to funnel-shaped or bowl-shaped depressions.

Earth on the Move

Sinkholes form when water dissolves underground rock. Rainwater or other runoff water mixes with **carbon dioxide** in the air and soil, making it slightly acidic. As the water seeps into the ground, it slowly flushes away soil and wears away rock. This **erosion** gradually results in larger and larger cavities opening up underground. Sometimes these cavities, or sinkholes, become so large they form underground caves.

Naturally formed sinkholes generally occur in places where the underground rock is soluble, or easily dissolved by water. **Limestone**, **dolomite**, and **gypsum** are the most common types of soluble rock. As the rock erodes and the sinkholes grow larger, the surface ground above these open areas begins to weaken. Whether the ground simply slumps slightly or crashes in without warning, it is because there is nothing underground to support the land's weight.

■ As water wears it away, limestone often changes into icicle-shaped formations called stalactites.

SINKHOLE DEVELOPMENT

1 Acidic water works down into the rock and begins to eat away at it. This makes small holes and tunnels in the rock. Soil falls into these holes.

2 If the holes are big enough, more and more soil will begin to fall into them, leaving empty spaces in the ground above the rock.

3 Over time, the holes in the stone get bigger and more soil falls into them, leaving an empty cave-like space in the earth above.

4 Finally, the roof of the hole can no longer hold up the weight above it. The roof collapses, bringing down everything above it. This is how a sinkhole forms.

Types of Sinkholes

Sinkholes vary greatly in size. The smallest are less than 3 feet (1 m) deep and 3 feet (1 m) across. The largest sinkholes may be steep-walled, gaping holes that measure hundreds of feet deep and hundreds of feet wide. Whatever their size, there are three main types of natural sinkholes.

DISSOLUTION SINKHOLES

- Most common and slowest to develop
- Found where limestone exists at the surface level, often barely covered by sand or soil
- Rainwater dissolves surface limestone, carrying it underground with the water.
- As limestone dissolves, shallow, empty pockets gradually form at surface level.
- These depressions often fill up with water, forming ponds or small lakes.

COVER-SUBSIDENCE SINKHOLES

- Form when soil or other loose ground cover material is not thick or solid
- Thin layers of sand or soil filter down into the **bedrock**, carried by water.
- Water works its way into cracks in the limestone, gradually dissolving it.
- Topsoil layer sinks in a bowl shape as **subsurface** limestone dissolves

COVER-COLLAPSE SINKHOLES

- Begin as subsidence sinkholes do, with water eating away at soluble rock
- Water continues to carve out larger and larger underground cavities.
- When the underground cavity becomes too large to support the ground above it, sudden collapse occurs.

Sinkholes created by human activity form differently. Most begin beneath city streets, where man-made "cave systems" contain countless pipes, such as water and sewer lines. If these pipes break, underground floods can happen, eating away at the earth around the pipes. Eventually, large holes form and the ground above them collapses, just like natural sinkholes.

■ When sinkholes occur in cities, they can be very destructive.

Sinkhole Areas

Sinkholes cover about 10 percent of Earth's surface. Most naturally formed sinkholes develop in areas of "karst" land. Karst is a type of **terrain** in which the bedrock is **porous** and soluble. Usually this porous bedrock is limestone.

In the United States, about 20 percent, or one-fifth, of the land is karst landscape. Sinkholes are especially common in Florida. There, nearly all the bedrock is karst. Other major U.S. sinkhole "hot spots" include Tennessee, Kentucky, Pennsylvania, Alabama, Missouri, and Texas. The Illinois Sinkhole Plain, in southwestern Illinois, is karst terrain. It has more than 10,000 known sinkholes.

■ The word "karst" comes from the name of the Karst Plateau, in Slovenia. Almost half of Slovenia is made up of karst, and the country has many sinkholes.

Sinkhole Timeline

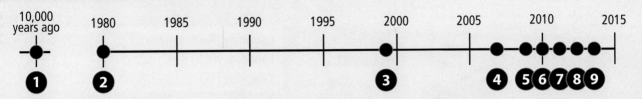

1   **2**   **3**   **4**   **5** **6** **7** **8** **9**

1 **10,000 years ago**
The last Ice Age ends. The Great Blue Hole, the world's largest **submerged** sinkhole, forms off the coast of modern-day Belize.

4 **2007**
"The Grandfather" opens up in Berezniki, Russia. It measures 1,289 feet (393 m) long and 781 feet (238 m) deep.

7 **2011**
A sinkhole collapses a busy city street in Beijing, China. It is likely caused by underground subway construction.

2 **1980**
A crew drilling in Lake Peigneur, Alabama, punctures the lake's bottom. The whirling sinkhole that results sucks barges and other equipment underwater.

5 **2009**
A sinkhole opens on a golf course in Tokyo, Japan. A 38-year-old woman falls 15 feet (4.6 m) to her death.

8 **2012**
In Assumption Parish, Louisiana, a 9-acre (3.6-hectare) sinkhole forms over a mining operation. The hole was still growing in 2013.

6 **2010**
A sinkhole destroys a house and three cars near Montreal, Quebec, Canada. The sinkhole covers an area larger than four soccer fields.

3 **1999**
The water of Lake Jackson, in Tallahassee, Florida, disappears into a sinkhole. As water level increases, the lake refills.

9 **2013**
In the central Florida area known as Sinkhole Alley, a large sinkhole opens up, taking a man's life while he is asleep in bed.

Sinkholes Around the World

ARCTIC OCEAN

Continent: North America
Location: Winter Park, Florida
Year: May 1981
Size: 350 feet (107 m) wide and 75 feet (23 m) deep
Fast Fact: $4 million in damage. Losses: 3-bedroom house; part of a swimming pool; five German sports cars at a dealership

San Francisco (2013)

PACIFIC OCEAN

NORTH AMERICA

ATLANTIC OCEAN

Dean's Blue Hole, Bahamas

Ik Kil Cenote, Mexico

Continent: South America
Location: Sarisarinama, Venezuela
Year: First spotted in 1961; first explored in 1974
Size: Four major sinkholes, the largest about 1,150 feet (350 m) wide and 1,000 feet (305 m) deep
Fast Fact: Sinkholes here are home to many plants and animals found nowhere else on Earth.

SOUTH AMERICA

N
W E
S

SOUTHERN OCEAN

LEGEND
⊙ SINKHOLES ★ FEATURED SINKHOLES ■ KARST REGIONS

SCALE
621 Miles
0   1,000 Kilometers

WHAT HAVE YOU LEARNED ABOUT SINKHOLES?

This map shows the locations of some of the world's major sinkholes. Use this map, and research online to answer these questions.
1. Which continent has the most sinkholes?
2. Why do sinkholes occur in these areas?

Samara, Russia (2005)

ARCTIC OCEAN

EUROPE

ASIA

Bimmah Sinkhole, Oman

AFRICA

INDIAN OCEAN

PACIFIC OCEAN

AUSTRALIA

Boesmansgat Sinkhole, South Africa

Continent: Africa
Location: west of Cairo, Egypt
Year: More than 5 million years ago
Size: Covers 7,000 square miles (18,100 square km) and is 436 feet (133 m) deep
Fast Fact: The Qattara Depression is the largest natural sinkhole in the world.

Continent: Asia
Location: Shenzhen, China
Year: 2013
Size: 26 feet (8 m) wide and 52 feet (16 m) deep
Fast Fact: A 25-year-old man was killed after falling into the collapsing sinkhole.

ANTARCTICA

13

All Fall Down

Sinkholes may occur naturally, but when they happen without warning, they can be a natural disaster. Sometimes there are warnings that a sinkhole is forming. Fresh cracks might show up in building foundations or walls. If a sinkhole has caused the frame of a building to shift, its doors or windows may not close properly. Cracks may appear at window corners. There might be cracks or sagging in the ground outside the house. Trees may start leaning. Another sign might be rainwater collecting in shallow pools in the ground where none existed before.

■ The Dead Sea, between Israel and Jordan, is rapidly evaporating, resulting in thousands of cover-collapse sinkholes along its coast. Every year, 200 to 300 new sinkholes develop there.

Inspectors can perform geological tests to detect sinkholes, sometimes using **ground-penetrating radar** or other equipment. Inspectors who check out these situations are often professional geologists trained to recognize sinkhole activity.

SINKHOLE SAFETY TIPS

- Watch for signs of sinkholes developing.

- Keep away from sinkholes, as they may continue to collapse.

- New sinkholes should be fenced off right away to keep people safe.

- Stay out of any building near a sinkhole until the building is declared safe.

- Never use a sinkhole as a garbage pit. Sinkholes often connect to sources of drinking water.

Sinkhole Myths

Cultures all over the world have myths related to sinkholes. Cenotes are a type of sinkhole that forms in the Yucatan Peninsula of Mexico. The Maya people of the Yucatan considered cenotes to be sacred places, and entire cities were built around them. Cenotes were a source of fresh water, but they also represented entrances to the underworld.

In the country of Oman, bordering Saudi Arabia, the Bimmah sinkhole is the source of one well-known myth. The story says that a chunk of the Moon fell from the sky, creating a vast hole when it hit Earth. Locals call this sinkhole *Bait al Afreet*, or "House of the Demon."

■ Cenote Ik Kil is one of the most famous water-filled sinkholes in the Yucatan.

Also from Oman is the story of Ubar, the lost "Atlantis of the Sands." The location of this fortress city remained a mystery for hundreds of years. According to legend, the city was sucked down into the sand as punishment for the people's dishonest lives. In 1992, the Ubar fortress was discovered. It had partly collapsed into a sinkhole. Scientists found that this sinkhole had once been a large underground cave partially filled with water. When the cave walls collapsed, the fortress went down.

In Greek myth, the prophet Amphiarius was fighting in a battle when the ground opened beneath him. Alive, he fell to the underworld. Zeus, king of the gods, gave Amphiarius eternal life to save him from the anger of Hades, the god of the dead. Hades was angry that a living man had entered the land of the dead.

■ The Bimmah sinkhole in Oman has become a popular tourist destination.

Mapping Risk

Geologists and other earth scientists use special instruments to look for sinkholes. One tool, the gravimeter, measures tiny changes in Earth's gravity from one place to another, in this case in underground areas.

When a cave forms deep underground in limestone, its gravity is slightly different than that of the surrounding rock. This difference helps geologists measure and map underground caves. In areas with karst landscape, scientists may drill below the surface or use **remote sensing machines** to map and pinpoint the location of sinkholes.

■ Geologists often use small remote control helicopters equipped with cameras. This allows them to see inside a sinkhole safely.

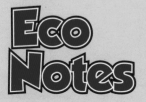

Gravimeters are not the only way to locate sinkholes. Geologists have many ways to inspect what is going on underground. Some techniques involve using underground radar or electricity to search for sinkholes. Computers analyze what the scientists find. Anything unusual may indicate a hidden sinkhole.

What is a Geologist?

Geologists are scientists who study Earth, its composition, structure, and the history of its development. Geologists also study how Earth changes over time, and what causes these changes. Hydrogeologists are geologists who locate and study aquifers, or underground water sources, in Earth. They also study the way groundwater travels through the rock and soil that make up Earth's crust, and how this water affects the land around it.

Daniel Doctor

Daniel Doctor is a research geologist with the U.S. Geological Survey. In 2006, Dr. Doctor began working with the Eastern Geology and Climate Science Center in Reston, Virginia. He has written papers on sinkholes, karst, and the effects of water on underground rock.

WORKING CONDITIONS
Geologists spend much of their time analyzing their findings in the lab. They also must work in nature when searching for sinkholes.

SAFETY
Geologists are not usually in danger of falling into a sinkhole while searching for them. However, they always work with caution. Their experience, detection equipment, and techniques help them understand the terrain and stay safe.

Seven Facts About Sinkholes

Drought and flooding can both cause sinkholes.

Some human-related causes of sinkholes include poor drainage systems and mining.

Sinkholes sometimes result in new water sources. Others reduce water resources.

Mexico's El Zacatón cenote is the world's deepest known water-filled sinkhole.

Sinkholes are also known as swallow holes and dolines.

Devil's Hole, Nevada, is the sinkhole home of the endangered pupfish.

Puerto Rico's Arecibo Observatory has its main antennae located in a huge sinkhole.

Sinkhole Brain Teasers

1 What are cenotes?

2 What is the largest known natural sinkhole in the world?

3 What kind of work do geologists do?

4 What are the three main types of sinkholes?

5 What are two other names for sinkholes?

6 What are the three most common types of soluble rock?

7 What was another name for the legendary lost city of Ubar?

8 Which endangered species lives in Devil's Hole in Nevada?

9 Why is it not always safe to stand on the edge of a sinkhole?

10 Where do most sinkholes occur?

ANSWERS: 1. water-filled sinkholes found on Mexico's Yucatan Peninsula **2.** Qattar Depression near Cairo, Egypt **3.** They study Earth's composition, structure, and history. **4.** dissolution, cover-subsidence, and cover-collapse **5.** swallow holes, dolines **6.** limestone, dolomite, and gypsum **7.** "Atlantis of the Sands" **8.** Devil's Hole pupfish **9.** It could collapse further and anyone standing nearby could be hurt. **10.** in areas of karst landscape

Science in Action

Make a Sinkhole

A sinkhole forms when water drains down from Earth's surface. Try creating your own sinkhole using soluble materials found around the house. Here's how.

Materials Needed

One box of sugar cubes
A package of graham crackers
A clear jar
Measuring cup
Turkey baster

Directions

1 Place a couple of graham crackers in the bottom of your jar.

2 Cover the crackers with sugar cubes.

3 Add two more layers of sugar cubes.

4 Cover the stack with crushed graham cracker crumbs. Press firmly to pack.

5 Slowly add water to the top of the stack using the turkey baster.

6 Watch how the sugar slowly dissolves.

Key Words

bedrock: the solid rock that lies beneath Earth's surface

carbon dioxide: a colorless, odorless gas that people and animals exhale when they breathe

dolomite: a soluble, translucent mineral closely related to limestone

erosion: the gradual wearing away of rock and soil by wind or water

ground-penetrating radar: radio waves that go into the ground and bounce back to a receiver when they hit certain types of formations, such as holes or caves

gypsum: a soft, soluble mineral, usually white or colorless

limestone: a soluble type of rock formed from particles that settle to the bottom of water

porous: full of tiny holes that let water pass through

predict: to say what might happen in the future

remote sensing machines: special machines often used to measure features, such as depth or rock thickness, through solid ground

submerged: underwater

subsurface: lying just below Earth's surface

terrain: land, especially related to the land's physical features

Index

Log on to www.av2books.com

AV² by Weigl brings you media enhanced books that support active learning. Go to www.av2books.com, and enter the special code found on page 2 of this book. You will gain access to enriched and enhanced content that supplements and complements this book. Content includes video, audio, weblinks, quizzes, a slide show, and activities.

AV² Online Navigation

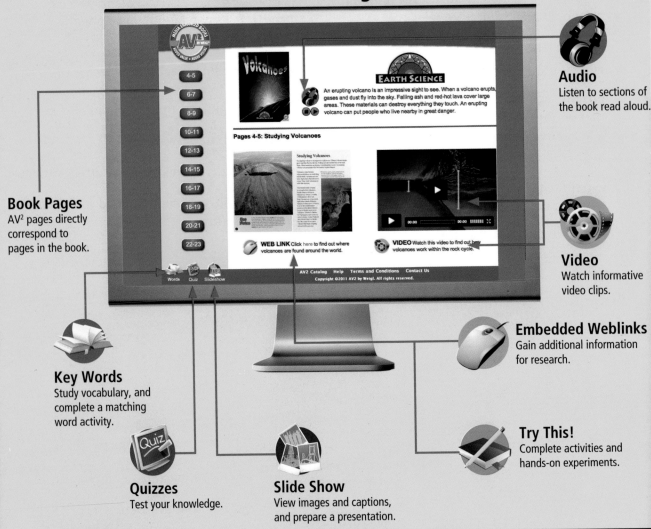

Book Pages
AV² pages directly correspond to pages in the book.

Audio
Listen to sections of the book read aloud.

Video
Watch informative video clips.

Key Words
Study vocabulary, and complete a matching word activity.

Embedded Weblinks
Gain additional information for research.

Quizzes
Test your knowledge.

Slide Show
View images and captions, and prepare a presentation.

Try This!
Complete activities and hands-on experiments.

AV² was built to bridge the gap between print and digital. We encourage you to tell us what you like and what you want to see in the future.

Sign up to be an AV² Ambassador at www.av2books.com/ambassador.